THE HATCHING OF THE HEART

The Poiema Poetry Series

Poems are windows into worlds; windows into beauty, goodness, and truth; windows into understandings that won't twist themselves into tidy dogmatic statements; windows into experiences. We can do more than merely peer into such windows; with a little effort we can fling open the casements, and leap over the sills into the heart of these worlds. We are also led into familiar places of hurt, confusion, and disappointment, but we arrive in the poet's company. Poetry is a partnership between poet and reader, seeking together to gain something of value—to get at something important.

Ephesians 2:10 says, "We are God's workmanship . . ." *poiema* in Greek— the thing that has been made, the masterpiece, the poem. The Poiema Poetry Series presents the work of gifted poets who take Christian faith seriously, and demonstrate in whose image we have been made through their creativity and craftsmanship.

These poets are recent participants in the ancient tradition of David, Asaph, Isaiah, and John the Revelator. The thread can be followed through the centuries—through the diverse poetic visions of Dante, Bernard of Clairvaux, Donne, Herbert, Milton, Hopkins, Eliot, R. S. Thomas, and Denise Levertov—down to the poet whose work is in your hand. With the selection of this volume you are entering this enduring tradition, and as a reader contributing to it.

—D.S. Martin
Series Editor

The Hatching of the Heart

MARGO SWISS

CASCADE *Books* • Eugene, Oregon

THE HATCHING OF THE HEART

The Poiema Poetry Series

Cascade Books
An Imprint of Wipf and Stock Publishers
199 W. 8th Ave., Suite 3
Eugene, OR 97401

www.wipfandstock.com

ISBN 13: 978-1-4982-0518-4

Cataloging-in-Publication data:

Margo Swiss.

The hatching of the heart / Margo Swiss.

viii + 78 p.; 23 cm

The Poiema Poetry Series

ISBN 13: 978-1-4982-0518-4

1. American Poetry—21st Century I. Title II. Series

PS3674.H535 2015

Manufactured in the USA.

To Dave and Jonathan
and
other friends and pilgrims

When our hearts are closed, we live within a shell.
To extend the egg metaphor: the shell needs to be
broken open if the life within it is to enter into full
life. What we need is the "hatching of the heart."
And if the heart is not hatched, we die.
(MARCUS BORG, *THE HEART OF CHRISTIANITY*)

Contents

1. A Thin Place

A thin place is the place where the boundary between heaven and earth is especially thin. It's a place where we can sense the divine more readily. (Celtic Tradition)

Photosynthesis

"The generative source of poetry is in silence and darkness."
(George Whalley, *The Poetic Process*)

From silence
the tidal curve of nothingness
this reckoning, stone with stone, falls
on sticks, on brittle tips of things.

A frill of light spokes and spears in air.
Touched by it, the barren trunks relent
melting, blaze luminous,
fire without heat.

Shaggy bulbs conceal their carpelled selves,
abound in sips, a shivery cool,
while sun with ranging ribs
breathes its light
engendering green.

God's Kinesis

"April is the cruellest month . . . ."
(T. S. Eliot, *The Burial of the Dead*)

The buds are breaking, biting themselves in sleep.
They wrestle interminably under winter scales.
It would be good to make light of pain as the buds do,
fighting for life on the inside
but it is too early for life.
It is a time of retention.
Green lives if only in the mind.

Taut in my season
there are two reasons for which I endure,
rivalrous as any green thing:
April blooms shooting through snow,
God's kinesis leafing in air.

Seeds

"every expression of the will of God is in some sense a 'word' of God and therefore a 'seed' of new life."

(Thomas Merton, *New Seeds of Contemplation*)

The hand that sows knows not
what seeds may grow, rise rife
with life, burrowing blackness
in God's own time to root, stem
and shoot together.

Nosing clean from ground's grave
they bear up bravely, eating earth away
denouncing dark with a blind might
in one last germinating gasp
break fast into morning light.

Living Water

(John 4.10)

Light rain—
soft, light rain rains.
Living water reigns.

Water
whether wanted
in storm

or warmed
still we are
watered

drenched
sometimes drowse
as roots

earthbound
feed, so we
night-long long

to rise
to rain
to fall as

light rain—
soft, light rain rains.
Living water reigns.

Spring Buds

In spring
buds are sentient, multi-ocular, perceive
light from everywhere.

Sun's air heats
sheaths hour by hour
melliferous cups, first filled,
swells that dermis
smaller than eyes can
accommodate to

burst, bloom.

Audience

Above all
this green
leaf-laden lushness
in that tree
I see
from where first
those double notes
burst.

The cardinal sings.

Red-suited
crowned
he a-warbling rings out
then double notes
again.

I am his
only audience
down here
lonely for the taking
ground bound
listening for
love's call.

I cry aloud, *again*
please, again!

He does so miraculously
then such a wonder-
ful life proclaim
rejoicing.

I stand below
and know
God too hears.

Dilatation

in summer
this tree
       is rain-soaked:
       black bark, the smell
       of wood, lightning-burnt,
       cutaneous, so that it hurts,
       green, so that it dilates
the eye
in summer

A Thin Place

(for my mother)

I'm just being quiet
the flat line of your lips
drawn over.

just being quiet. . . .
after years of war
(long forgotten).

> The lash of events against
> her six-year-old scapulae—
> made to strip bare before
> hands tore flesh, a blur of
> eyes and teeth, unleashed to
> drive the point home—
> the little upon the least.
>
> Later, in the bath
> her welts blister and burn
> raw to the touch,
> after long hot days when bladder scalds
> from dehydration of summer sweat
> and too many tears wept
> so her eyes swelled.
>
> Or night commands to
> *shut up your coughing:*
> her throat ached, trying to,
> trying not to
> flinch in the way of
> drunken curse or
> hand slug in the face:

don't you dare
talk back.

One ragged sleeve of pain
worn inside out
so none heard
the scream, rolled up so tight
she'd need to bite down
to swallow the cry whole,
felt like
forever. . . .

One day
the angels came
woke her breathless
whispering her name:

a day so heavenly
        everything
                for a time
                        slowed
                                down

(heart beating in her mouth)
saw sun rise
burst into her eyes
such a large fair green place
space enough to stand straight up in—

And then
she said, *mommy,*
I've seen God!

Sunflowers

"and there is nothing hid from the heat thereof."
(Psalm 19.6)

God's Sun
flowers flames green-gold
lines gone forth out of Him—

takes truants a-sudden
hauls holds steady
heart to heart—

rends not garments
the will clean clothed anew
in the sheer mercy-might of Him—

then
fires again
even greater gold—

       the heat thereof
       being His
       only.

Manitoba Trees

Poplars aglow surely know of times to come,
simply throw themselves into life—
reckless as lovers, reel sideways
skyways, any way, agile beyond belief
every leaf angling, spun in sun
awash with light
in spite of *dry heat.*

What does it mean
that these brave trees seem eternally bent upon
such a vast chloroplastic blast
long to outlast their first June greening
too soon cast down, silvered
under God's own eye?

May we never forget
their photosynthetic rush against all odds
how weathering harsh storms they warm
(for a time) even these dull-rooted
winter-ward hearts
they bow to.

On the First Anniversary of My Father's Death

We caught fishes in your favourite pond and you said it was a secret
place where nobody else came so after you got sick you even talked
about buying it just to have somewhere peaceful to go and it had bush-
es all around and underwater stems and roots that used to tangle in my
reel and you were always quiet when we fished and said we shouldn't
talk except to make signs for worms and new hooks so we'd sit waiting
all afternoon with me dreaming and once when it was cloudy and cool
I thought it was the kind of day when something wonderful might
happen but I didn't say it out loud because you'd just keep staring out
at the water and after awhile we got out of the boat and moved care-
fully along the edge watching for trout and I told you I didn't like the
speckled ones because they had a strong taste but you said that being
dark their meat was more nourishing so we fished for them off a small
dam and I remember not knowing what to do when I hooked one so
you grabbed my pole trying to keep him on but he swam away and I
walked off into the bushes where it was greenest after the rain and I
liked the green because it was easy to look at and smelled good and
soon you forgot the fish so I think now we were a lot alike because
you often walked by yourself in your knee-boots taking long strides
through the grass and sometimes you'd go out early and come back
saying it was a perfect day for sunning because it was a little overcast
and I was never sure why that should be but it seemed natural for you
to be right because you understood more about the sun and sky than
anyone I knew but when I go over all my memories I think most often
of watching you from the kitchen window last April walking in the
back field before the buds came out and even though seeing you there
is still clear on my mind the worst part is being alone and remember-
ing the pain of looking under rocks and bushes after your hard dying

2. The Taking of a Grief

*(17th Century usage: "to sustain
great loss; receive a wound")*

The Taking of a Grief

When bad news comes
are you ready
to receive it head on, or
do you strike a distance,
wear a disguise, body armour
or some other mode of defence?

Do you stand your ground
like an antique hero
or assume your position
like a lawyer in court?

Are you at such times
reasoned, or
do you just let go
let come what will
straight to the heart

the full frontal thrust of
the absolute *must*
of what will be:
        in then out
        with your blood on it?

How shall you live
knowing such grief
in a moment
and nothing else for certain
except
time does not always heal?

Budgie

When our budgie started to get old dad and I used to clip his beak
because it grew horny and curled under and tangled in the cage wall
and he'd squawk till we came to unhitch him and I'd hold him easy
in my hand and his eyes looked like scared rings while we did it and
so last spring when dad was dying he turned yellow and grew claws
something the same way fumbling around with everything and I was
the only one he wanted because he knew I'd helped the bird before so I
used to take his hands that were like sleepy things because they had no
feeling in them and I'd trim off the dead nail being really careful and
I even did it the day they stopped growing altogether and it was awful
because there was more dead in him than living and I wished I could
say all kinds of things while I did it because we'd never talked much
and he used to hold on so tight you could tell he'd take me with him if
he could and I'd have gone too because after that I tried hard to make
it there myself but then I got better so now I've got my own nails to cut
just like the rest of the stuff you have to do when you're moving around
keeping the dead part under control

Her Body

(for my mother)

Her body is outstretched on disinfected sheets,
its nakedness exposed by the gloved compassion of a nurse.

Uncovering wounds:
frozen years ago
her right shoulder protrudes,
its humerus cap absorbed—
in life cut
bleeding beneath skin.

One breast flattened by time,
the other excised, its scar faint,
give no account of shame
or the loss of *perfect breasts*
preserved with care after childbirth.

Her slender waist and unflawed belly
betray no signs of struggle
of love, either feared or forced,
of threats sustained,
the defeated parting of thighs
that proceed now in silence
from two surgically-pinned hips.

And what of this luminous
eighty-six-year-old skin
stretched lineless over all
as blood empties its way softly,
descending down to feet
twisted and blackening?

This tissue memory of tears
is sealed forever.

Her profile remains
dauntless
with aquiline intent.
Eyes wide
peer upward
to where
she lingers a time
to behold her self,
transfigured ageless,
in full morning light,
no longer needing
candles or moon
to guide her.

On the Death of My Mother

If I could
I would be the archangel
(lily in hand)
would gladly say
the very words
to re-annunciate your birth
and pour you perfect
into the world.

I would bring you forth
a new creation
from God's hand
his Grace descending
stroke by stroke
to that sacred place
on which
I would set the crown
for which
you have always longed
so that
when you arrived
breathless and blind
emptied of dreams

I could give you back
life.

Elegy for Aunt Anne

You told me how
people had taken your house
        that you had wanted
        to give to us
        but
people had taken your house
they had taken your house.

A doctor
        who was a very mean man
had taken it over
        there
where sick people stayed
the house was full
        now
of sick people
being cared for
        by somebody else
        by somebody else
in your own house.

Upstairs too
there were people who
were dancing
        upstairs
people dancing
        all night
        laughing
and you did not know
        who
        or where
to go next
        so

you took a taxi to town
            to see
            your brother
where
the sky was as blue
as your father's eyes
            you said
you remembered everything
but had no one.

And I remember you
old for a very long time
in your own house
surrounded by
newspapers and dust.

I loved you forever before that
and even after
you drove me away.

But today we meet again
with tears running down
kiss and cry together
we say
            so much
            we've missed
            so much!

Message From Carol

(For Sr. Carol Lindholm)

When we spoke of the showing,
the veil of the passion
stretched tightly over your face,
you exulted in the thought that
it was a sign of his love.

In time
your tumored lips and phlegm-clogged throat,
blocked as by a stone,
broke the silence
with a cry for deliverance
from the tomb you had become.

Yet at the very last
you slipped out like a dream
as we slept.

Later you called back just to say,
It's Carol, everything's all right now!

Wisdom's Work

(For Lillian Dauphinee)

*"Although she [wisdom] is but one, she can do all things . . . in every genera-
tion she passes into holy souls and makes them friends of God, and prophets."*
(Wisdom of Solomon 7.27)

You would walk to the bus
three more times before you died
(if only we had known).

You always dressed with care:
hair in tidy curls, blouse with brooch inset,
that spritely step and lusty laugh.
You did not look your age
or seem so very wise
as God had made you
who gave you eyes
to see into our hearts.

Remember once, beside the Lady shrine
you drew that callous hand of mine
back to back against my enemy's,
broke our grudge in two (before we even knew)
wisdom's work had joined our selfish selves
to make them gently bend.

Valentine Presence

(for Ruth, February 14, 2010)

You turn   smilingly say   *I love you*
eyes half-closed   as the sound slips
still warm from your lips   words heard
as for the first time.

I see you there as never before
your once buxom health devoured by age
with life bearing down on us both,
a fine pair we make reciting our creed:

> you barely able to stand and
> me barely able to see through the tears
> of this heart-piercing grace.

Women Tell

Women tell of their babies who died:
ones born black as your boot, grey or blue
ones who lived just a day or two
ones who slept with death in their cribs
ones who were spindly and could never suck
ones who were taken before they wore clothes.

Women tell of the nurseries they made:
linens and lamps, assorted notions of joy,
the patient passing of nine months gone
as on a long trip, heavy with love for the unexpected
to be finally rejected by somebody special
who never arrived, a door slammed in the face,
the place they came to a vacant space,
a house abandoned and all swept clean
with only a single sign on the door,
no body lives here any more.

How Could They Know?

(for Tony, July 15–17, 1977)

How could they know
when I told them *something was wrong*
or how awful it felt to have you
there under my heart those many months knowing
that *something was wrong?*

How could they know
that your little nub of a lung had gone
virtually undetected along
with that diaphragmatic hole that let
your tiny bowel float freely up
into your chest?

And how could they ever know
how beautiful you would finally be
when at last you came to me, arms open like Christ's
before they cut the cord
to break us both in two?

Or how blindly I searched for you, after,
hands kneading nothing at all
but slackening flesh and bone

                alone
                in hospital dark?

Sacrifice

(for my sons Anthony and Jonathan)

"Mom, let's say a prayer,
say a prayer. . . ."

There
in an evening church,
day's light emptying
upon the bowed head
of my living son—

    suddenly
    appearing
    from ten years back,
    his newborn nape;
    I am weak
    with the brush
    of love's
    cheek—

        see
        my firstborn's eyes
        locked ceilingward
        wide with the dread
        of his two-day life.

        On my belly
        that hour
        could he,
        palms open to God,
        know
        he would not live,
        and in leaving give

place
to his brother
over whose crib one day
there would hang a rainbow

above whose head
now at prayer
the banner reads:

Blessed is He who comes
in the Name of the Lord?

3. Ascent

In darkness, and secure,
By the secret ladder, disguised,
Ah, the sheer grace!
(St. John of the Cross, *The Ascent of Mount Carmel*)

Lover's Instructions

Lights out
now step into the dark
lift up your eyes to whatever
you can not see.

As the blind go
so you must move
hands in reach of whatever
you can not know.

Here
even fear recedes
and words
fail.

Beyond
in silence
Love stands ready
(eyes closed in anticipation)
to cover you
with such an embrace.

In this place
all receive
and none waits.

Here Now

"I am here and not not-there"
(Margaret Avison, *An Autobiography*, 145)

No need to ask
where we are going
when

we are there
all the time.
Here

I am (says God)
but are you
listening?

No More Music?

"Sing unto the Lord a new song"
(Isaiah 42.10)

Some have said that in our post modern
post-structuralist age
lyric utterance is dead
so there ends the music.

But can they prove it?
Do they really mean
that between you and me
there can be no more music?

Why not go all the way and say
day has only begun
and the sun is young enough for us
to weave, word by word, a new song
for here and now to show how
Love's feet, formerly pinned,
leap free, athletic and trim,
to hurdle the world
and never once limping?

Do they really think
that after all these years we still drink old wine?
We whine ourselves, lyric-lonely as any,
the only difference being
we raise antiphons of praise
even on bad days.

We cross our hearts and hope to die if we,
who caused the cord to strike so long ago,
dissonant and dumb, are not this day
the chord that sings
aloud in Him.

Prairie Flower

I meet you blistered
petalled Christ, morning crowned,
enduring day-long the searing sun
yet still not dead.

Tomb you burst from,
the sanguine mother, earth
you pry through
your unsoiled beauty
martyred to this dull world
steams the eye veins.

Witness now
how even the hard heart
breaks.

Temptation

"And Jesus being full of the Holy Ghost returned from Jordan, and was led by the Spirit into the wilderness, Being forty days tempted of the devil."

(Luke 4.1-13)

He blooms best in rocky places
words like weapons
unarmed otherwise
mans himself—

pinned in converse
stands the point
compassed round by
bread and stones and temple roof—

wins the day
unlocks the door
unknots our sorry
sickly selves—

turns the tables
tears the veil
breaks the serpent's head
though his is still unpillowed—

bursts alive
in Father-flames
frees forever
all men.

Meditation On A Franciscan Crucifix

Thunder cracked
rattling his lungs
so hard-pressed to stay standing
Francis cringed beneath the opulent voice
that smoked him clean out into the wilderness.
He went and walked there
until his heart burst.

At first he thought
the shock too much
feared to undress his adolescent skin
draw in, release
the ultimate raw exhalation
that stripped him
naked before God
so shelterless
he wandered
day and night
grew then thin for Him,
could no longer speak.

Over his head
all the while spread wings,
he saw with awe how feathered and furred things
nosed their way into his flesh,
picking and licking his wounds
till bathed clean by their tongues
he shone.

Later in the town
whoever eyed his limbs,
gleaming with light, would say,
have pity on the lad.
And they covered him
with the skins of animals.

It followed therefore
he would fashion his life
after such poor creatures
gentle as himself who,
nailed many nights ruthless by Love,
stands forever poised
on two bloody bare feet.

Cross Examination

"experimentum crucis . . . *the test, the 'experiment' of the cross, the way in which, in our own self-understanding, the cross tries and probes us."*
(Rowan Williams, *Christ on Trial*)

Cross examine us, Lord,
by the rigor of your Word;
rase bright with your light
our closet-dark hearts
that when called to confess
we awaken to see
how once upon a tree
You died.

That verdict of shame,
exposing our sin, condemns
(so help us God)—
and the same by issue of grace
commends
(both just and true)
your merciful turning us in
to You.

Ascent

Sun-gone
winter branches are bared by wind.
Nowhere to hide—

Turn back then
(head bowed to weather)
ascend this lonely hill
where once seated on grass
you caught a blond son's smile
tossed over a shoulder—

suddenly
   down   comes a
      convoy   of carriages
         spilling   over
              wheel   upon wheel
                  descending   what
                      mystic   pour of
                          mother   tongues
                              eyes   wide with
                                  joy   flash flood of
                                  love   tearing
                                    the heart open to
                                    seize   a rude
                                        comfort—

now   at least   you know the way   home

The Glance

"When You looked at me,
Your eyes imprinted Your grace in me;"

(St. John of the Cross, *Spiritual Canticle*, 32)

I set my heart upon you, Lord,
this very day
my only hope a solitary ray of light
so bristling-bright
it fires the fainting heart in me.

Now raised to life,
just one glance from your sweet eyes
looks me out of pain.

Divine Economy

"Since thou wast precious in my sight . . . I have loved thee."
(Isaiah 43.4)

Take me, Lord,
poor
as I am
and for my debt
make me more
poor,
till poorest
I become

no more
than a mere mite
of my self
no credit due
that wholly spent
can only be
redeemed
in You

accounted true
and precious
in your sight
to live
love-changed
within
your dear
treasury.

Fisher

"Follow me, and I will make you fishers of men."
  (Matthew 4.19)

Man fishing:
windward reels
currents shifting
tow to beach-break
waters in.

Man fishing:
lures to light
calloused hands, eyes
peer beyond in
carnal daze.

Man fishing:
fears the depth
swollen tongue, sun
parching, breaks his
beggar's heart.

Man fishing:
trawls the dark
weeds, sinks to where
a drowned pilot once
lost, now walks.

   God's Body:
   is forever
   baiting, waiting
   enthralling, draws
   the good catch.

Wrestling with God

Is that you, Lord?

Who *am* I   wrestling with?   One
flick of the wrists   lays me
flat   heart to heart   though
all my might's bent   dead-set
against him. . . .

Would you quit your flapping, girl!

Now all my wind's gone   sink or swim
He's got me   either way
we're both done in

Those gut-deep cravings gotta go, girl
frisk down to skin   rinse away sin
like winnowing   didn't I tell ya'?

A sinking ship   scuttling
foundering   to the depths
me cold in the hold   Him hard at the wheel
turning us   inside out   forever

at his mercy   then
nothing
but Him

Easter Conversations

"they said unto them, Why seek ye the living among the dead? He is not here,
but is risen: remember how he spoke unto you when he was yet in Galilee."
(Luke 24.5-6; 10-11)

Jesus Christ knows flesh,
bodies speaking, always did
do what his Father said.

His mother's hard labour, first,
in time, his own: walked his talk, then
was crossed, tombed, shut up for good
dead (it was said)
until

He heard his Father say, *rise,*
be born again this day.

"It was Mary Magdalene, and Joanna, and Mary the mother of James,
and the other women that were with them, which told these things unto
the apostles. And their words seemed to them as idle tales, and they
believed them not."

4. The Hatching of the Heart

Companionship is for the hatching of our hearts . . . for the bringing home of our scattered and fragmented selves, for the making of a heart at home with itself. When I am at home with myself in God, I can then be truly present to my friends and fellow pilgrims.

(ALAN JONES, EXPLORING SPIRITUAL DIRECTION)

St. Thomas's, Huron Street

"The wounded surgeon plies the steel
That questions the distempered part;
Beneath the bleeding hands we feel
The sharp compassion of the healer's art . . . ."

(T. S. Eliot, *East Coker*)

Our holy home stands
soaked in the smell of sacrifice.

Sun *plies* light-hallowed air
splitting dark where
Christ himself hangs,
a lonely agony of eyes
by *sharp compassion* spent.

His valiant grief
now beaten glorious,
breathes a wonder
like the heart
in a surgeon's hand.

Do You Love Me?

"Jesus said to Simon Peter, 'Simon son of John, do you love me?'"
(John 21.15-17)

One dark night
bedded down with death
that none might see
the wreck of wounds I was,
a stone upon my heart

> I died I thought
> then heard
> a simple word
> *do you love me?*

All night and day the sound of busy sweeping
filled my brain, swept away the rot, remains
of hope and dusty dreams of love
worn down by dread despair
and sickness unto death

> I dreamed, I thought
> then heard
> a second word
> *do you love me?*

As I slept, one bowed his head
longed, He said, to start my heart
again, lips to ear, pledged all
his love to ask
one final time

do you love me?
Then I
replied
I do.

Little Girl

In morning
a little girl waits
naked, small
fists clenched in
fright
at a bedroom door.

Shoulders locked
body taut
she stands
alone
bathed in more
than sunlight.

Milk of Saints

She had thought it might mean death,
            that dream—
her father, beside her bed
vigilant as never in life,
her mother, no longer bent with age
standing beneath her window
calling her name—

In time she spoke plainly to Him,
conceding possible defeat
offering the most she could give
knowing the way to be narrow
the gate straight.

Then into the silence
He roared his answer
bristling the roots of her hair.

Blood ran cold and
eyes teared to hear:

>   *As a courtesy to you*
>   *and for your protection*
>   *I have taken you into my heart*
>   *that I may nurse you*
>   *on the milk of saints.*

Mother God

On hands and knees before you, God, I fall,
bear with grief this wretched beggar love.
Face down dead I lay
the once soft heart You worked in me
turned now so sickly hard
that hardening harder still
is doomed to kill
my light and life.

The sin I bring devours my rest
eats and burns within
yet wears itself without
by such disguise as otherwise
seems meet and right.

How shall I find You now, O Saviour God,
in this sick parching heat?

A desert land extends no hand to spare
what further shame I fear:
your mighty rod that reigns
to break the back of my desire
to be your constant child.

Become, dear Christ, instead, my Mother God.
Exchange this brutal love that bends
for one that raises up,
that You, once soiled for me,

shall call this breach a necessary sin
to lead me home
and by my own
poor nakedness in You
redress your glory, Lord.

Mary's Hands

(for Maria Belka, massage therapist)

Mary's hands are all
I need now.
Her voice and
lamb-like face
recede.
Hands alone
and only hers
become God's upon my shoulders,
now uncrossed,
perform their act of mercy
to transubstantiate my grief.

God's body once undone
became itself a burden
to be taken down
swallowed by death
yet rose,
so mine,
world-weary and worn,
is hosted by one who
bearing love in his Name
assumes my pain.

She is Mary
gentle tender of wounds
by whose strokes
I am healed.

The Hatching of the Heart

"For ye are dead, and your life is hid with Christ in God."
(Colossians 3.3)

Stoned by sin and left to die,
I wore in heart, as One passed by,
a bloody thorn, *worn in grief,* He said,
for both our sakes, then bore
such heavenly holes in every door
I'd set to close on Him—

Yet passing through
as He might do, He soon undid
the vain disguise my shame devised,
before my very eyes prepared instead
to dress me best in Him,
assumed, He claimed, *the sin,*
and stripped himself
to walk with manly Grace the rocky way
He vowed I needn't take.

When all was done,
He gowned me fresh in his sweet flesh
and hung around my neck
his gentle, broken heart
to which He prayed I'd learn to
listen close and well.

So dearly won,
my brittle heart began to break
to hatch itself a little one like his
that draws its life from his open side,
where newly-born in safety now
in God himself we hide.

Incarnation II

"he sings in my mouth, like a heart outside of me,
hoping i will appear as he, the one incarnation that marries me"

(Pier Giorgio Di Cicco, "Marrying God")

my
dear
Lord

only You know   how cold I grow
to my very toes   in dire extremities

too soon
presume
forget

then
pretend
to love

defiant still   deny with will
how sure I am   how true You are

and ever
shall
be

bone
of my bone
and
flesh of my
flesh

Light Delivery

(for Dr. Melanie Caetano, Obstetrics & Gynaecology)

Pregnant with worry these many months
I've grown gut-heavy with gloom
though friends have prayed,
nay-sayed with conviction
all shall be well.

And to meet at last
this brave slip of a girl who welcomes first,
then hands me inside and out
with her true-touch fingering! How cheerfully
she probes my morning dark, invites
this tongue-tied heart to bear down and express
its full-term delivery of grief.

I marvel in light
of her expert articulation
of this brisk benediction
that summons with such ease tears of simple joy
from these bone-dry eyes.

Outside after
high over everything I see
that rain has cleared,
that sun, drawing back curtains of cloud,
has finally broken through
swabbing streets clean
awash in noonday light.

God's Pleasure At St. Thomas's
Out of the Cold/Heat Programme

"Verily I say unto you, Inasmuch as ye have done it unto one of the least of these my brethren, ye have done it unto me."
(Matthew 25.40)

It's quite a procession when it starts
not exactly communion but very orderly,
bags open, not hands, take sandwiches
each signed by its maker—

>   *beef   turkey   tuna   cheese   salmon*

eyes down, the file past is solemn

>   *fruit's in the middle*
>   *water's at the end.*

Not much shame in these folks
but we're awkward.
It's hard getting used to this
because *we're all hungry.*

The piano rolls out some old tunes.
A dog roams the room,
mixing in where we can't,
wagging anywhere just for a touch
from anybody   anytime   for a minute even.
Dogs give unconditional love
gratefully passing their bodies around
loosening hands and hearts
spreading Grace
better than we can.

He's here alright
eating with the rest of them,
mostly men, just a few women.
He's used to that where he comes from.

He's pretty inconspicuous,
goes around with them everywhere.
He might even have belted a few back himself
before they came over for the food.
Remember they called Him a drunkard
in his day?

He's definitely here now.
You can't tell which one He is,
always keeps a low profile.
But He's out there
with the rest of them.

The line forms to the right.
            Ice-cream's the best!
They come like kids to a corner store
taking whatever we give and gladly—
scoops not quite round
cones not always full
some running down.

This slow frenzy of treats
gets us all going, everybody
face to face, joining eyes like hands together,
shy smiles melting into each other,
tasting something wholly sweet stirring down deep and
licking us clean all over
plain giddy with the gift of it—
            when
            Somebody
            somewhere
            laughs right out loud!

Jonathan's Liturgy

In the beginning
we strolled mindlessly on air
afraid of everything, though no one knew
how much you gave me hope.
We arrived and departed, baby-faced, synonymous,
passing in and out daily until age
and ambition slipped between us.

I loved you then without fault,
knew the pain of which women speak:
They grow up so fast. . . .

Today in a gesture of help
you reason symmetrically
like the man you will become
correcting my distress by simple fact:
It's here, Mama! Here. . . .

May there be more prospect before us
than merely peace at the last
and what we remember so differently
if at all.

Vigil Blessing

I find you sitting at five-years old,
gentle-eyed, a kindergarten teacher by your side,
enduring on humble children's chairs
(in knitted hat and boots)
the wait I have imposed upon you.

Eager to leave on Christmas break,
a thousand working mother's jobs to do,
she remains behind, instead, with you,
the last child in the class, longing
for holidays and fun, yet joined now as one
in this solemn bond of patience.

Three o'clock passed
as snow begins to fly
your faces, vigil-set, betray no aggravation or regret
just hope respectively contained,
the tender joy of mouths and eyes of glad reception.

At my graceless spilling over of excuse
forgiveness only nods and smiles.

Maternal Eros

(For Jonathan)

Before you entered the world
God knew you perfectly;
you were to Him
as though His only one.

Yet loving
(in His way) unjealously,
He gave you to me
to harbour wholly
unseen.

Bathed in dark
you grew, in time to pursue
your gallant path to light:
infant, boy, adolescent and
before me now

    a man
    standing fast
    in God's footsteps.

    I joy for
    love of
    you.

Good Friday Sleep

Your voice fades into a yawn so wide
as to swallow whole the pillow
on which you fall
asleep. . . .

Nothing is
more true than you drifting through
the clean soul-space of God's Almightiness,
his Grace billowing
infinite.

Hours later
you remember only waking to a start,
hoping day had finally come.

Still dark with dreams
you bravely dare
strip bare the altar of your heart,
slide again into night
till morning breaks
at the rising of the sun.

Love's Looking

Sun on leaves
shimmers in   shadow light
silk-seeming stems
whip windy   then
still.

Boughs brim green   flame
in leaf kinesis   pulse
tears too   blind
(for a time) till
all clears.

He loves
this   our   awed   lost   looking
heart-eyed

bears down   burns
clean hot
for us.

Rapture

"The eternal God is thy refuge. . . ."
(Deuteronomy 33.27)

To think
He'd seize me   rebounding against his will
                barely holding on   until
                his rare heart-to-heart speaking
                tightly braided into my brain

                sets free
                lets me
                live again

to hear
that   still   small   voice
washing clean over all that
refutes   denies   turns
sickly pale   and dies
for a time   lost

now found   safe
beneath *the everlasting arms.*

Apology

(for Dave)

One dark night a year later,
when you had not arrived home
at the predictable hour,
I imagined the worst
on a long black road—

Only then did I know
how it had been for you
(now safely under my hands)
as I heard your cries again:

    You can't leave me!
    You can't leave me!

How you must have waited,
numb as the nights between the days
you walked through, parade of appearances,
in your deferential way mouthing obligatory words,
prayers unceasing for his unfathomable Grace,
feared for a time drowned in one dark pool
round which not a single stone was left
unturned.

Only now do I see
how the bitterest part had to be
my coming back with tears and grief,
but no apology.

Evening Walk

(for Dave)

The path we have followed
(not always of our own design)
leads us at an evening hour
to these Japanese cherry trees.

Their blossom canopy floats above
a blessing in any tongue.
You are my dearest love
steadfast as the arm I hold.

We are heart-weary tonight.
Sun sets, showering pink
into branches of gold.
Beautiful, we say,

it could be morning
even.

Acknowledgements

I offer my deepest gratitude to the divine Author who inspired and guided my hand. I also thank my husband Dave for his steadfast support and insightful suggestions; Don Martin, my meticulous editor, for tidying and polishing the text wherever necessary; and my son, Jonathan Kent, an interested observer of my writing and the "trigger" for some of these poems. Thanks also to Susan McCaslin for years of encouragement and her inclusion of "Audience," "Sacrifice," "Lover's Instructions," "Meditation on a Franciscan Crucifix," and "Divine Economy" in her anthology *Poetry and Spiritual Practice* (The St. Thomas Poetry Series, 2002.)

I am grateful to Hannah Main van der Kamp who generously solicited twenty of these poems for inclusion in her chapbook series. *Here Now* was published in Powell River, B.C. (Arkwark Press, 2012). My special thanks to Stuart Isto for his fine production and design.

Thanks also to Todd Swift for selecting "Mother God" for his anthology, *The Poet's Quest for God* (London, England: Eyewear Press, 2014).

My appreciation as well to John North for including "Easter Conversations," "Love's Looking," "Here Now," "Mother God," and "Women Tell" in *Love, Knowledge and the University: Essays and Poetry from the Christianity and Literature Study Group, Victoria, 2013*, ed. John S. North (Waterloo, ON: North Waterloo Academic Press, 2015.)

Poems previously published in periodicals include the following: "Budgie" *(Quarry)*; "On the First Anniversary of My Father's Death" *(Far Point)*; "Jonathan's Liturgy," "Her Body," "Mary's Hands," "A Thin Place," "Mother God," "Women Tell," "Maternal Eros," "Light Delivery" *(Canadian Woman Studies)*; "Sunflowers," "Apology" *(The Antigonish Review)*.

COLLECTIONS IN THIS SERIES INCLUDE:

Six Sundays toward a Seventh by Sydney Lea

Epitaphs for the Journey by Paul Mariani

Within This Tree of Bones by Robert Siegel

Particular Scandals by Julie L. Moore

Gold by Barbara Crooker

A Word In My Mouth by Robert Cording

Say This Prayer into the Past by Paul Willis

Scape by Luci Shaw

Conspiracy of Light by D. S. Martin

Second Sky by Tania Runyan

Remembering Jesus by John Leax

What Cannot Be Fixed by Jill Baumgaertner

Still Working It Out by Brad Davis

Collage of Seoul by Jae Newman